TABLE OF CONTENTS

ACRONYMS

UK	United Kingdom
UN	United Nations
US	United States

TABLES

CHAPTER 1

INTRODUCTION

<u>Background</u>

Terrorism and democracy make an interesting dichotomy. Political rhetoric from recent and present world leaders link the spread of a strong democracy with a decline in the number of areas that are capable of producing and harboring terrorists. George W. Bush stated in his inaugural address that "The survival of liberty in our land increasingly depends on the success of liberty in other lands. The best hope for peace in our world is the expansion of freedom in all the world. . . . So it is the policy of the United States to seek and support the growth of democratic movements and institutions in every nation and culture, with the ultimate goal of ending tyranny in our world" (Bush 2005).

Totalitarian regimes are often characterized by their lack of terrorism, and if they do encounter terrorist acts their laws and system of government often allow them to expend great resources without needing to consider the rule of law, or basic human rights to seek out the perpetrators. The Nazi regime, the KGB, Iraqi secret police, and more recently the military junta in Burma have all been successful in finding, publicly punishing, and suppressing terrorist acts within their borders (Lutz and Lutz 2010).

Terrorism is not a new phenomenon but for many people it was only recognized when the two airplanes crashed into the World Trade Center in New York on 11 September 2001. This act of terrorism, committed by the terror group Al Qaeda, saw the beginning of the Global War on Terror. Al Qaeda is based in the Islamic religion, and when coupled with the subsequent wars in the Islamic countries of Iraq and Afghanistan, lead many people to identify terrorism with the Islamic faith. Recent history,

1

expeditionary conflicts, and friendly military deaths have kept the public focused on Islamic religion based terrorism.

While populations and governments of Western democracies have been focused on fighting terrorists in other countries and building security measures around their own countries, to prevent the people they are fighting from committing another 11 September style attack, there have been incidents of birth right or homegrown citizens adopting terrorist tactics to attempt to influence, change, or collapse the government from within the state. This study will present three case studies to highlight the threat from citizens adopting terrorist tactics within the state, and how some of the rights of the citizens within that state can assist a homegrown terrorist in hiding their true aims and objectives, while preventing law enforcement from detecting possible threats until it is too late.

The first case study will be that of the little known cult, Aum Shinrikyo and its leader Shoko Asahara. In 1995 it announced itself by killing 12 people and injuring thousands by releasing Sarin nerve agent into the Tokyo subway system. This organization was not based on Islam, nor did it arise in the Middle East. It did, however, use terror as a method of spreading its message. While much of the focus is on the organization itself, its actions and the associated consequences, its leader, like Osama Bin Laden, Aymen Al-Zawahiri, and Muqtada al-Sadr, is portrayed as the primary driver behind the terrorist act. Asahara "spent much of his pre-adult life in a state-run boarding school for the blind. His feelings of abandonment by his family, discrimination because of his blindness, and later failure to enter a university left him with permanent feelings of rejection, frustration, and resentment" (Bromley and Melton 2002, 192).

The second case study challenges the notion that the threat from terrorism is required to be associated with either religion or a Middle Eastern Country, or have roots in an extremist ideology. Timothy McVeigh and his attack on the Federal Offices in Oklahoma City is an example of an attack by a person who identified himself with his country and considered himself to be very patriotic (Green and Alexander 1995). His patriotism was skewed to the point that he thought the United States (US) was under threat from its own Federal Government. McVeigh was raised in a Catholic household and his father was a devout follower of Catholicism. McVeigh himself did not identify with any particular faith, and did not have the stereotypical family upbringing of a stable family consisting of two parents who nurtured and mentored him; he was largely raised by his grandfather. McVeigh was linked to the militia group, Michigan Militia, but was not considered a violent person by those who knew him.

The third and final case study will be the London bombings in 2005. This case study is important to balance the three studies in the thesis. The London bombings represent three birth citizens and one naturalized citizen carrying out an act of terror against their home country under the banner of Islam. These bombers were all raised in relative religious freedom and some were even described as rejecting their religion in their teenage years, although all identified with Islam at the time of the bombings. For these men their participation in society led some in the community to express disbelief that they were responsible for these acts of terror (BBC News 2005).

Terrorism is the emerging threat to security in the post Cold War Era. For many, predominantly Christian countries that maintain a Western style of democratic rule, terrorists are framed as largely originating from areas in the Middle East, as young men

3

from "fundamentalist organizations, social protest groups, and radical political movements, both of the left and the right" (Michel and Herbeck 2001) and who have been radicalized by extremist Islamic religious leaders.

Primary Research Question

Are there aspects of democracies that shield homegrown terrorism from detection? The recent conflict in Iraq and the current conflict in Afghanistan have given rise to a perception amongst some areas of Western society that all terrorism is based on Islamic ideology. Conjecture in the media and political rhetoric when discussing conflicts suggest that terrorism is a product of religious radicalization of Islam coupled with a failed state apparatus that cannot support a common rule of law.

Given the experiences of homegrown terrorists executing attacks against the Tokyo subway, Oklahoma City and the London bombings what aspects of democracy, individual conditions, and individual psychology allowed them to commit these acts against their own nation states.

Subordinate Research Questions

What were the origins of the groups and individuals which were involved in the incidents in Oklahoma, London, and Tokyo? How much influence do external factors have over an individual's involvement in a terrorist act? Do democracies need to change to reflect a terrorist threat?

Significance

This research is significant in attempting to correct some social fallacies about the nature and predominant religion involved in terrorism. By choosing three case studies which do not fit into the stereotype of terrorism, it is hoped that individual and social conditions are seen as an important attribute, as well as religious fundamentalism.

By identifying the social and individual conditions that are common in all three case studies and analyzing their effect on the terrorists, it may be possible to identify particular groups through social mapping and apportion of resources to that area. Identification of certain behaviors and traits of individuals from school age could also be used, to show a correlation between childhood and adolescent experiences and the possibility of committing a terrorist act.

Identification of civil rights are providing more flexibility than others for a terrorist to function within a domestic environment, and allow for impartial analysis of possible factors that could be changed to eliminate the loop hole, which protects terrorists and their operations.

Limitations

This thesis is limited in that any linkages that are made will not be absolutes and cannot be applied across all examples of terrorist acts. The use of three geographically different case studies is meant to present a cross section of different acts, which like the World Trade Center attacks, ignited public debate on the topic of terrorism.

This thesis will not address the interaction of effects between the conditions that exist within the democratic state, individual conditions, and individual psychology. There is not enough time to draw comprehensive and well supported comparisons between all areas of the studies in an attempt to predict the exact set of conditions that cause individuals to commit acts of terror.

Individual conditions and individual psychology will not be discussed in detail against the three case studies. The case studies will be assessed against the conditions set by a democratic state only. This will limit the overall scope of the study to the primary research question.

Religion and its links to radicalization and Middle Eastern states will not be discussed in detail. The radicalization and involvement of Islam and other religions is important as it relates to religious protection underneath a democratic society, but its role in non-democratic states will not be discussed.

The role of Aum Shinrikyo will only be discussed in relation to the events that occur in Japan. It is acknowledged that the religion had many other followers in the US, Australia, and Russia and continues to be active, but this is beyond the scope of the thesis as it is the actions of the democratic state of Japan and where the actual terrorist acts that were committed, that is to be discussed.

This thesis is limited to three case studies only. Due to time constraints it is not possible to discuss any more than three case studies in depth. The case studies are deliberately picked for their distinct differences of effect, location, ethnic makeup, and time in order to demonstrate some similarities in acts of terror.

Definitions

Terms defined as part of this thesis are described below. These are the manner in which these terms are used within the context of this thesis.

Democratic Society. Is defined by the United Nations (UN) General Assembly as "a universal value based on the freely expressed will of people to determine their own political, economic, social and cultural systems and their full participation in all aspects of their lives" (United Nations General Assembly 2005).

Principles of democracy. There are seven core principles outlined by the US Department of State, they are: Sovereignty of the people; Government based upon consent of the governed; majority rule, minority rights; guarantee of basic human rights; free and fair elections; equality before the law; due process of law; constitutional limits on government; social, economic, and political pluralism; values of tolerance, pragmatism, cooperation, and compromise.

Basic Human Rights. Are defined in accordance with the UN Charter on Human Rights (The United Nations General Assembly 1948).

Rights of an individual. Are defined by the UN as:

1. The right to legal recourse when their rights have been violated, even if the violator was acting in an official capacity.

2. The right to life.

3. The right to liberty and freedom of movement.

4. The right to equality before the law.

5. The right to presumption of innocence until proven guilty.

6. The right to appeal a conviction.

7. The right to be recognized as a person before the law.

8. The right to privacy and protection of that privacy by law.

9. Freedom of thought, conscience, and religion.

10. Freedom of opinion and expression.

11. Freedom of assembly and association (The United Nations General Assembly 1948).

Radicalization. This definition is from Mr Charles E. Allen in his written testimony to the US Senate when has was the Assistant Secretary for Intelligence and Analysis, and the Chief Intelligence Officer of the Department of Homeland Security, in 2007. Radicalization entails "the process of adopting an extremist belief system, including the willingness to use, support, or facilitate violence, as a method to effect societal change" (Allen 2004, 4). This definition separates radicalization from terrorism by emphasizing the difference between related social patterns, some of which may eventually lead to terrorism.

Terrorist. An individual who commits, attempts, or wishes to commit an act of terrorism (see definition for terrorism).

Terrorism. The following definition is taken from the UN Security Council Resolution 1566 "Criminal acts, including against civilians, committed with the intent to cause death or serious bodily injury, or taking of hostages, with the purpose to provoke a state of terror in the general public or in a group of persons or particular persons, intimidate a population or compel a government or an international organization to do or to abstain from doing any act" (The United Nations Security Council 2004).

Structure of the Paper

The first chapter presents the topic of the thesis in the form of a research question and subordinate questions. The background to the problem is presented and why it is significant enough to warrant further study. This chapter also outlines the key limitations in the research, which allows for the research to be further defined and allow for the possibility of further research in this area. The final piece to the first chapter is the definitions that are required to understand the context of the research.

The second chapter consists of the literature review. The review centers on the sources of research that have been obtained for the thesis, with a comparison on what others have deduced from their research into similar questions.

The third chapter is the methodology. It outlines the qualitative case study analysis of the three case studies, and the use of these to inform my research question.

Chapter 4 will be the analysis of the case studies. The evidence gathered will be presented, explained, analyzed, and interpreted. The interrelationships in the research will be discussed and compared against the research question.

The final chapter, chapter 5, will state the discoveries made from the interpretation of the research evidence. The significance of the results will also be discussed within the field of study and recommendations for further research will be made.

CHAPTER 2

LITERATURE REVIEW

The literature review will focus on four main areas of contributing research; the discussion on whether democracy promotes terrorism; the literature on the 2005 London bombings; the literature on Timothy McVeigh and the Oklahoma bombings, and the Sarin gas attacks on the Japanese subway, by the Aum Shinrikyo cult.

The literature will be grouped into areas to generalize similar findings and topics and will answer three main questions in relation to the literature. What do we already know in the immediate area concerned? What are the characteristics of the key concepts, main factors, or variables? What evidence is lacking, inconclusive, contradictory, or too limited? This literature review will be summarized by answering the question: What views need to be (further) tested in relation to each of the four areas explored?

Democracy and Terrorism

There are two major perspectives that are prevalent when discussing the effect of democracy on terrorism. The literature is roughly divided equally between the two opinions; that democracy does promote terrorism and that democracy does not promote terrorism. Many of the authors listed in the literature attempt to use quantitative data to prove their point but their data and definitions are too diverse to compare to each other.

Brian Jenkins and Timo Kivimaki break democracy down even further to look at the aspect of law and its effect on the citizens (Jenkins 2010; Kivimaki 2007). Jenkins asserts that the role of law enforcement and their inability to cope with acts of terrorism due to their structure and consequence management approach is their main problem. Law enforcement does not utilize a preventative approach; rather they are inhibited by the civil rights enshrined within democracies. These rights do not allow law enforcement to conduct unfettered, full scale domestic intelligence collection on citizens (Jenkins 2010, 8).

Similarly Kivimaki states that the rule of law and law enforcement is the most continually visible form of democracy and can act as a possible motivating factor of terrorism. The hunt for terrorist entities in either an actual or potential terrorism incident can cause immature democracies to disintegrate. The implied and promised protection that a democracy provides is often violated in the name of protecting it (Kivimaki 2007, 50-53).

James Lutz and Brenda Lutz offer a slightly different view in their research which focusses on terrorist incidents throughout the world between 1972 and 1995 (Lutz and Lutz 2010). This research does not find a direct correlation throughout the entire world but does find results in different regions. In some regions, such as the former Soviet territories and China, there is a very low rate of terrorist related incidents but that could be because terrorist incidents are not reported. In other areas, such as the Middle East there is a high rate of terrorist attacks. The article concludes that law enforcement is a definite factor, as are social freedoms amongst the citizens and that terrorism is more likely under a democracy (Lutz and Lutz 2010, 68-72).

Quan Li presents empirical data similar to that of Lutz (Lutz and Lutz 2010) in his discussion of democracy promoting transnational terrorism (Li 2005). Li states that democracies do promote transnational terrorism and that it is the civil liberties present in a democracy that protect the terrorists. Li argues that in some cases the institutions themselves are the reasons for the terrorism, and that the protections they guarantee to citizens of that society actually undermine the overall fight against actual and potential terrorist organizations (Li 2005, 294). Li and Drew Schaub present another article (Li and Schaub 2004) where they link the lack of integration in a globalized economy, to the spread of terrorism. The economic freedom and participation that is guaranteed under a democratic government is globalization. Li and Schaub assert that the lack of globalization leads to poorer nations and the ability for terrorist groups to disenfranchise the populace against globalized democratic nations. They conclude that democratic nations should be contributing economically to poorer nations, to see them reduce the population resource to terrorist groups (Li and Schaub 2004, 252-254).

Peter Kurrild-Klitgaard, Mogens Justesen and Robert Klemmensen find that "small" amounts of democracy (as is present in immature states) initially allows for terrorism to flourish but as the concept and embrace of democracy grows within the populace the level of terrorism decreases. Unlike Li and Li and Schaub (Li 2005; Li and Schaub 2004), Kurrild-Klitgaard, Justesen and Klemmensen find that there is no data to support economic status of an area being linked to the amount of terrorist activity originating or controlling that same area (Kurrild-Klitgaard, Justesen and Klemmensen 2006, 308-313).

Erica Chenoweth and Nahla Shahrouri argue that terrorism is promoted through democracies but only because of the mobilization process of the political arena and the need for groups to compete against each other (Chenoweth 2010; Shahrouri 2010). Shahrouri uses quantitative data to demonstrate that there is a correlation between terrorism and democracy (Shahrouri 2010). Chenoweth states that democracies will be

12

tempted to alter their rights and freedoms to counter the threat of terrorism but should resist the urge to do so, instead they should seek to extinguish the competition between groups and seek ways to infiltrate them, to enable their destruction (Chenoweth 2010, 26-28). Shahrouri argues a similar understanding but raises the risks of forcing democracy upon a nation as a possible cause of terrorism in the future (Shahrouri 2010, 67-69).

Michael Freeman and James Piazza offer a contrary view to the subject (Freeman 2008; Piazza 2007). Freeman argues that the spread of democracy is the main cause of terrorism because the spread of democracy threatens the four main areas of global Salafi terrorism. Military, economic, political, and cultural reasons are all areas where terrorists believe there is a threat from the spread of democracy and an undermining of their core beliefs, which in the case of this article is Islam (Freeman 2008, 40-43). Piazza believes that the spread of democracy to the Middle East will create terrorism, as the causes of terrorism are too numerous to be covered by the single solution of democracy. He goes on to argue that immature democracies can easily become failed states which are breeding grounds for terrorist groups (Piazza 2007, 536-537).

David Kibble in his article "Is Democracy a Cure for Terrorism? A Review of Natan Sharansky's The Case for Democracy: The Power of Freedom to Overcome Tyranny and Terror" is emphatic in his agreement with Sharansky's singular argument for the spread of democracy to undermine the roots of terrorism (Kibble 2006). Kibble does, however, deviate from Sharansky and aligns with Piazza (Piazza 2007), Li and Schaub (Li and Schaub 2004) when he agrees democracy alone cannot be the only cure to terrorism and that underlying economic problems must also be addressed (Kibble 2006, 389-390).

The final article for this section of the literature review is by Konstantinos Drakos and Andreas Gofas. This article relates to the underreporting and manipulation of quantitative methods by the various researchers and authors, to attempt to prove their particular view point of whether democracy does or does not promote terrorism. Drakos and Gofas argue that societies should set agreed parameters and then quantitative methods should be adopted, to prevent the use of non-standardized parameters being utilized to prove a certain theory in relation to terrorism (Drakos and Gofas 2006, 732-734).

The works cited throughout this section of the literature review are best summarized by Drakos and Gofas (Drakos and Gofas 2006). Broadly, the works attempt to summarize or find definitive reasons behind democracy and its link to terrorism, by using set definitions or quantitative methods. Almost all attempt to include all terrorist incidents within a date range across the entire globe. There is little or no acknowledgment that democracy is different between nations or that the definitions of democracy and terrorism differ so greatly between the authors.

There is ample opportunity to generalize in this area and not be drawn into making definitive conclusions about a permanent link between democracy and terrorism. A possible area for further research is to clearly analyze the relationships of difference parts of democracy against the growth and spread of terrorism, in relation to the three specific terrorist case studies.

7 July 2005 London Bombings

Raffaello Pantucci outlines the history behind the current Counter Terrorism approach in the United Kingdom (UK), analyzing its origins and the move away from the domestic threat of the Irish Republican Army and towards the 1980 to 1990 imported threat of Islamic Jihadists (Pantucci 2010, 251-254). Pantucci discusses the failure of the UK Government policy in the wake of the 2005 London bombings, including its ongoing failure to outlaw the Hizb ut Tahrir group, which claimed responsibility for the attack (Pantucci 2010). Pantucci is limited in his research as he does not answer any of the questions that he poses about the quandary which exists, when governments attempt to respond to public opinion by promising tighter controls but are hampered by their own citizens not wanting any restrictions on their civil rights.

A newspaper article by the BBC, "Suicide bombers' 'ordinary' lives" summarizes the lives of the four bombers (BBC News 2005). It provides a succinct account of their history that is able to be easily digested. In contrast, the book by Malin Rai (Rai 2006) provides an in depth look at the bombings from a variety of sources. Rai analyzes the supposed public opinion and attempts to link the involvement of the UK in the Iraq War, to the radicalization of the four bombers.

Rai offers a very comprehensive view of the 7 July 2005 London bombings but is very vigorous in his attempt to link the Blair Government and Iraq directly to the bombings. The presentation of the bomber's lives and their descent into radicalization is well portrayed and provides an excellent analysis for the case study (Rai 2006).

Paul Tumelty in his article for the Terrorism Monitor (Tumelty 2005) is very similar to Rai (Rai 2006) but provides a more in-depth article than the BBC synopsis

15

(BBC News 2005). Tumelty is very factual and does not attempt to link the bombers to an underlying cause like Rai and the Iraq War (Rai 2006) but does comment on the future of the UK Counter Terrorism policy and the future of UK born Muslims. Tumelty provides a short by well researched and factual article that will balance some of the assertions made by Rai.

Aidan Kirby asserts that the type of terrorism seen in the 2005 London bombings is not just homegrown but is a new form of terrorism called "self-starters" (Kirby 2007, 246). Kirby claims that at risk individuals align themselves with a well-known terrorist organization and then emulate their actions using their existing knowledge without formal assistance or links. Kirby analyzes the official UK Government report into the 2005 London bombings and looks at why the attacks were not able to be thwarted by domestic security agencies (Kirby 2007).

Kirby does not give an in-depth look at the bombers or into the actual acts themselves, focusing more on the aftermath and control measures put in place by the authorities to prevent further attacks. Kirby does look at the broad threat of radicalization in the UK that played a part in the bombings, particularly the rise of the internet (Kirby 2007, 425) and the social and economic problems of minority groups (Kirby 2007, 422). The absence of a detailed analysis into the life of the bombers by Kirby will be covered by Rai (Rai 2006) who provides an exhaustive account of the bombers in a domestic context.

The book, *Understanding Violent Radicalization, Terrorist and Jihadist Movements in Europe* is a series of edited essays by Magnus Ranstorp that detail the growth and spread of radicalization (Ranstorp 2010). The essays focus on Europe and detail the early lives of the four bombers and their motivations, unlike Rai it does not seek to draw linkages to causes (Rai 2006) but does provide more background into Jihad and radicalization in general within the UK. The Ranstorp essays are factually sound and offer more amplifying information than Kirby (Kirby 2010) or the BBC article (BBC News 2005) and are a good contextualized account of radicalization in general within the UK and broader Europe.

There is not a large amount of literature available about the 2005 London bombings which is partly due to the recent nature of the attack. The information that is available is well researched and covers the incident in detail. Between the BBC, Rai and Kirby there is enough information to provide an accurate case study of the four bombers and their terrorist act. Some of the literature has an obvious bias (Rai 2006) which will need to be carefully accounted for and separated from the case study. There is more than enough research to conduct the case study and there is no current analysis against democracy, which makes it a candidate for further study.

<u>Timothy McVeigh and the Oklahoma Bombings</u>

Michelle Green and Brian Alexander write a brief, pretrial commentary on McVeigh in their article "Shadow warriors" and also briefly cover his upbringing, post military life, and connections to right wing militia groups (Green and Alexander 1995). This article provides useful background information and provides interesting details of his friends but does not go into the detail required; it also does not draw any conclusions and is merely a factual account of a limited section of McVeigh's life.

In Barbara Ehrenreich's article, "The making of McVeigh," a small portion of it extols McVeigh for the politically correct language he used in his justification for the bombing against the US Government (Ehrenreich 2001). Ehrenreich also provides a brief account of McVeigh's life, similar to that of Green and Alexander (Green and Alexander 1995) which focusses on McVeigh looking for answers and being drawn to fringe groups. The Ehrenreich article will have limited utility in the overall thesis but will allow for a greater understanding of the groups that he gravitated to. Ehrenreich herself provides a large amount of bias against the Federal Bureau of Investigation and the US Government specifically and this will have to be separated from the facts, before presentation within the case study.

Dick Reavis presents an interesting article from his position as a witness for the defense in the trial of McVeigh titled "Understanding Timothy McVeigh" (Reavis 1997). Reavis was called as a witness to comment on the influence that literature about the Waco incident could have had on McVeigh. McVeigh has cited the Waco incident as an important event that had affected him in his defense and Reavis had written an authoritative text on the incident. Reavis offers a brief view of McVeigh and focusses more on Waco, the US Government, and the supposed impartiality of the press (Reavis 1997).

The Reavis article provides a very small amount of important information on a key event in the life of McVeigh; he takes the Waco siege and contextualizes it from the defense counsel position. There remains a large amount of bias in the article but it does provide important information into one event and its affect on McVeigh.

Rage on the Right: The American Militia Movement from Ruby Ridge to Homeland Security, by Lane Crothers, clearly states that there is no "silver bullet" in a person's upbringing to suggest that events in childhood or adolescence will cause an individual to commit an act (Crothers 2003). Crothers skims much of the early life of McVeigh and centers on the period when McVeigh was linked to a militia movement, attempting to draw comparisons away from other causes and relate the reasons for the attack on the militia and racism (Crothers 2003, 128). This text contains some bias against the possibility of lasting mental impressions being formed in childhood through experience but does not present evidence to support this premise.

The Crothers work does give valuable insights into the US militia movement and into racism in general, as well as the time that McVeigh spent in the US Army. This text will prove useful in the case study when looking at McVeigh as an adult.

Lou Michel and Dan Herbeck provide an informative account of McVeigh in their text *American Terrorist* spending a great deal of time discussing the childhood, adolescence, and eventual terrorist act of McVeigh (Michel and Herbeck 2001). This text goes into much greater detail than that of Ehrenreich (2001) or Green and Alexander (1995) about the early life of McVeigh and some of the influences that may have had a lasting effect on his life.

Unlike Crothers (2003) and Reavis (1997), Michel and Herbeck do not attempt to lay singular blame on any one event, or attempt to provide a singular cause as the reason why McVeigh committed the act. The account by Michel and Herbeck remains factual and when combined with the previous listed works will form a large part of the case study.

Stephen Currie provides a narrow synopsis of McVeigh in his book *Terrorists and Terrorist Groups*, preferring to skim many details of his life in favor of writing about the actual act, the trial, and the events leading up to death of McVeigh (Currie 2002). Currie lacks sources in some of the assertions he makes and draws some major conclusions relating to McVeigh's time in the Army, especially when discussing unfounded and unreleased psychological documentation (Currie 2002, 61). Currie does discuss some of the potential danger signs that were exhibited in his time in the Army but does not build upon this evidence. This gives cause for further research into this area.

Some of assertions made by Currie are confirmed by Michel and Herbeck (2001) and Crothers (2003) but others fall into hear say. Currie will be useful to fill in some aspects of McVeigh's military life, that are not well covered by Michel and Herbeck but caution about the accuracy of the information will be required before using it as a potential source.

Like Crothers (2003) and Reavis (1997) Stout attempts to lay singular blame on childhood factors, most notably McVeigh's parents. Chris Stout also asserts that war trauma was to blame for the Oklahoma bombing and could have been averted. Similar to Crothers (2003) there is a lack of referenced source material in the work by Stout and much of the work seems to be an opinion rather than fact. This work will be useful from a psychological perspective when dealing with the case study, but any assertions it makes will require it to be carefully checked, due to the lack of references it contains.

There is much work on McVeigh but little which discusses his early life and upbringing. The main source of information in this area will come from Michel and Herbeck (2001) who have a well-researched text that deals with his early life. The other articles and texts are roughly similar in content but tend to either provide too much of an overview, such as Green and Alexander, or attempt to draw conclusions or set parameters without supporting research (Crothers 2003; Reavis 1997; Currie 2002).

There is ample opportunity for further study in this area, as the authors have not looked at democracy and its traits against the act McVeigh committed or the reasons why his behavior was not identified earlier.

Aum Shinrikyo and the Japanese Subway Attack

Daniel Meraux's journal article "Religious Terrorism in Japan: The Fatal Appeal of Aum Shinrikyo" documents the rise of many religions in Japan and broadly separates them into two groups, the ones that began post World War II and those that began in the 1970s to 1980s (Meraux 1995, 1141). Meraux notes the relatively modest beginnings of Aum Shinrikyo and outlines the criminal acts that they committed, under the cover of a religion (Meraux 1995, 1140).

Meraux provides a good analysis of the Shoko Asahara, the leader of Aum Shinrikyo, cataloging the rise of both of the religious cult and the leader to commit the fatal attack in the Tokyo subway (Meraux 1995). Meraux does conclude that Aum Shinrikyo is a criminal organization, although he notes that its 10,000 followers do not agree and that it was granted religious status under Japanese law (Meraux 1995, 1143).

The text *Blood That Cries Out From The Earth*, by James Jones, gives a well referenced account of the early beginnings of the Aum Shinrikyo religious cult and unlike Meraux (Meraux 1995) does not focus on early crimes committed by the leadership (Jones 2008).

Bruce Hoffman provides a much broader overview and focusses on the beginnings and growth of Asahara himself in his book, *Inside Terrorism* (Hoffman 2006). Hoffman considers Asahara in a more global fashion, examining his followers, growth, and paranoia to outside influences (Hoffman 2006, 118).

21

Hoffman is the only source who provides details of Aum Shinrikyo's early attempts at terrorist acts (Hoffman 2006, 124-125). While Hoffman does not link these directly back to democracy, he does comment on the actions taken by government figures and organizations in the wake of these acts. Hoffman, when linked with Jones will prove much of the information for the case study and the analysis in chapter 4.

Jones also offers an early portrayal of Asahara and focuses on the incidents that occurred and how his behavior changed at the same time. While detailing his behavior, the teachings that Asahara delivered are also analyzed to see their change in message, against the change in the social and political pressures places on Aum Shinrikyo at the time (Jones 2008, 74).

Jones discusses the links between Asahara and Aum Shinrikyo and the how the decline of one is directly linked to the decline of the other (Jones 2008, 85). This leads Jones to analyze parts of Asahara's early life, to determine what his motivations and disabilities were and how society in general treated him. Jones links the pursuit of spiritual renewal with a destructive path, to explain the actions of Asahara and Aum Shinrikyo (Jones 2008).

Jones will provide much of the information about Aum Shinrikyo and Asahara, as his text is well researched and comprehensive (Jones 2008). The article by Meraux provides excellent insights into the criminal dealings of Aum Shinrikyo (Meraux 1995) and will be used to amplify the comments made by Jones.

The most detailed and thorough account of Aum Shinrikyo and Asahara is the book written by Robert Lifton, *Destroying the World to Save It: Aum Shinrikyo, Apocalyptic Violence, and the New Global Terrorism*. Lifton discusses, in a detached and analytical way the theory and teachings of Aum Shinrikyo and how they appealed too ordinary citizens (Lifton 2000). Lifton also spends a great deal of time explaining the desire to own large amounts of highly destructive weaponry and the theory behind how and why it was to be utilized.

At the end of the text, Lifton provides an insightful and thought provoking comparison of Asahara and McVeigh and what would have happened if the tools which were readily available to McVeigh, were available to Asahara. In addition to this, Lifton hypothesizes on the future of groups like Aum Shinrikyo and where they are heading.

Lifton provides an excellent source of material on Aum Shinrikyo and will be used extensively throughout the case study. The other texts will be used to fill in details, add specifics, and check the facts of Lifton.

As detailed within the literature review there are gaps in the current research that are open to exploit. The majority of the research focusses on a requirement to blame someone or something, rather than analyze what contributes to the problem. Democracy itself is often looked upon as a definitive problem or solution and not merely as something that may contribute more or less to a particular situation. The definition of democracy is also unilaterally applied to all nations in the case studies, without acknowledging the variations between them; I believe this has led to a skewing of the results in some areas that may have led to incorrect conclusions.

Throughout the literature review it has become obvious that attempting to link quantitative data, such as the number of attacks in a given time period against a certain geographical area, to prove a particular point, is not conducive to providing a balanced argument. This narrow approach to the data does not take into account the political situations or the presence of inter or intra State conflict at the time of the studies, also all the studies listed did not take into account poor recording and reporting of such incidents in non-democratic countries, like the former Soviet Union or China.

This thesis will limit its scope to three case studies which take place in geographically separate areas. These isolated incidents will provide a broad cross section of homegrown incidents which will then be analyzed, to examine if the presence of a democratic government either assisted or hindered the terrorists in committing their acts.

CHAPTER 3

METHODOLOGY

Purpose

The purpose of this study is to examine three distinct case studies; the 2005 London bombings, Timothy McVeigh and the Oklahoma bombings and the Sarin gas attacks on the Japanese subway by the Aum Shinrikyo cult. The organization of chapter 3 presents the methodology used to research the purpose of this study. This chapter describes the presentation and application of the methodology used to present the case studies and the analysis of the information in the following chapters. Much of the literature in this topic comes from case studies which attempt to link quantitative data, such as time periods against the number of attacks in a geographical area. These case studies fail to address the wider non qualitative causes that also contributed to the attacks and their conclusions are narrow and incomplete. This study will look at three case studies and offer recommendations as to whether there are aspects of a Western style democracy that contribute to terrorist acts against it.

Case Studies

A case study is the study of an issue that has specific boundaries attached to it, to limit its scope, define its approach, and to establish the context (Creswell 2007, 74). Multiple sources of information and multiple case studies are utilized to provide an in-depth analysis of a case over time or through different scenarios, that provide a controlled medium for answering the research questions. Case studies themselves can be identified by the size of the case, how many subjects the case study involves, or the overall intent of the actual case study. There are three distinct variations with the intent of a case study: the single instrument case study, the collective or multiple case studies, and the intrinsic case study. The collective or multiple case study is the method that will be used in this research, as there is a single underlying idea and three case studies presented to prove or disprove this idea.

The most important part of a case study is setting the boundaries and limiting the scope of the case studies, this important step was completed in chapter 1 with the definition of the primary and secondary research questions. The use of the three case studies will dilute the complexity and the level of analysis to be undertaken, which is a risk but to support or offer confirmatory evidence, there needs to be some form of generalization (Creswell 2007, 74). This generalization will attempt to show any correlation across three societal, time, and geographically different case studies, which will assist in answering the primary research question. A table will be utilized as a means of consolidating the information, to aid in the readers understanding of the three case studies and how they are limited against certain criteria.

The three case studies to be discussed are clearly distinct, both in geographical area, terrorist backgrounds, and time periods. The primary research question poses the question, if democracy can be partly responsible for the resulting actions of the case studies and if the rights that are held to be inalienable for the majority of Western nations can be used to prevent detection of and even encourage radicalization of the perpetrators.

The Oklahoma bombing shows an attack against the US Government by a citizen that considers himself to be "more" American than other citizens and has even fought for the US in the 1991 Gulf War (Currie 2002). McVeigh offers a unique insight into someone that considers himself to be defending his country, and race, and even the democratic system against his perception of evil.

The Aum Shinrikyo cult also considers itself to be a defender of its own faith, a religion, but does not harbor the same intent to save others as McVeigh did. Their use of democracy and the principles was never more evident then when they attempted to become part of the process as a political party (Jones 2008).

The 2005 London bombings show a mix of religion, radicalization, racism, and democracy that offers a comprehensive picture of a homegrown terrorist threat. This case study is important as it is a modern day example, which mixes the primary research question of homegrown terrorism against imported terrorism, based on religious affiliation.

All three of the case studies will be compared against the principles of democracy that is defined in chapter 1. By holding all three to account, against the same democratic ideals in all three nations (all three nations are signatories to the UN Human Rights Declaration) the case studies will be able to present which, if any, aspects of democracy assisted or dissuaded the perpetrators of the terrorist acts.

Table 1 will be the table that will be used at the end of each case study to analyze if the required rights existed in each case and if the rights were exercised by the terrorists. The table is not weighted as the rights are not mutually exclusive of each other; they overlap and complement each other. The lack of weighting of criteria also prevents a numerical analysis of the results being extrapolated from the data, even if a group used only one right to shield its activities, it will provide insight into the primary research question.

A check or cross will denote if a right was used by a terrorist or terrorist group, knowingly or unknowingly to shield their activities from authorities and the population. If the right is not applicable to the case study an explanation will be provided as to why it is absent in that particular case study.

Table 1.   Comparison of Democratic Principles Against the Case Study (example)

Serial	Criteria	Oklahoma City and Timothy McVeigh	Aum Shinryko and Shoko Asahara	The London bombings and Mohammad Sidique Khan, Shehzad Tanweer, Germaine Lindsay and Hasib Hussain
1	The right to liberty and freedom of movement.			
2	The right to equality before the law.			
3	The right to legal recourse when their rights have been violated, even if the violator was acting in an official capacity.			
4	The right to presumption of innocence until proven guilty.			
5	The right to privacy and protection of that privacy by law.			
6	Freedom of thought, conscience, and religion.			
7	Freedom of opinion and expression.			
8	Freedom of assembly and association.			

Source: Created by author.

CHAPTER 4

ANALYSIS

Aum Shinrikyo and Shoko Asahara

On 20 March 1995 a nerve agent, known as Sarin gas, was released on five morning rush hour commuter trains in the Tokyo subway system. The gas was concealed in small bags carried by male members of the Aum Shinrikyo religious sect and at a predetermined time were punctured by sharpened umbrellas. The aftermath was 12 people dead and 3,796 injured (Jones 2008, 71).

Shoko Asahara

The self-professed guru of the cult was a legally blind man who was born in 1955 to a poor family of tatami craftsmen, in the Kyushu provisional area. He was known as Chizuo Matsumoto and had glaucoma, which left him completely blind in one eye and partially blind in the other. His parents enrolled him in a school for the blind where he found himself the dominant member of the student body, largely due to his partial sight and his physical size over the other students (Lifton 2000, 14).

Asahara would be considered the classic bully by today's standards. He would use his physical advantages over other students and force them to fight each other, often beating students who did not perform to his expectations. Asahara would openly rebel against his teachers; sometimes challenging them with physical violence, although he would quickly back down once challenged and deny that he was provoking a confrontation (Lifton 2000, 14).

Asahara had a poor but relatively normal Japanese upbringing, especially when considering his disabilities. He was further marginalized within the Japanese culture, he was known as a *burakumin* or village person. This was a derogatory name given to Korean immigrants. While the effect of this racist term is unknown, Asahara did use it in his teachings to highlight how he had succeeded in the face of adversity (Lifton 2000, 15).

Asahara seemed to be obsessed with two things in his life when he was growing up, money and drama. Asahara was an avid entrepreneur and loan shark, requiring payment from other students to conduct tasks that he was able to complete, due to his relative advantage of limited sight. He also avidly watched television dramas and acted in plays, eventually writing his own play about a prince and playing the lead role himself. At several points during his time in school he attempted to run unsuccessfully for head student position and despite handing out candy for bribes was still beaten (Lifton 2000, 15).

At the age of 12, Asahara left the school and moved on with his life keeping with him the lessons that he had learnt. While the teachers had taught him well in his studies he took with him his knowledge of fear, manipulation, and extortion that he could gain from people who depended on him.

Upon his graduation in 1975 Asahara became an acupuncturist and masseur in Kumamoto and practiced in this field for a year, before he had his first encounter with the law. In 1996 he was arrested for causing bodily injury to another person, found guilty and fined for the offence. Shortly after he moved to Tokyo and continued to practice as an acupuncturist while reading and studying the writings of Mao Zedong (Lifton 2000, 17).

Asahara met, had a child with (she would have another five children with him) and married Tomoko Ishii in 1978. Her family was moderately well off and provided him with a Chinese herbal medicine business. The business was a great success and Asahara was able to make a lot of money but in his quest to make more he took short cuts and was arrested, convicted, fined, and bankrupted in 1982 for selling fake medicines. Asahara continued with his study of Mao's writings and attempted to master traditional forms of fortune telling and anything connected with divination and mysticism (Lifton 2000, 17).

Asahara joined one of the new religions named Agonshu in 1981. The term "new religion" relates to any religion in Japanese society that was created after 1814 and has roots in prewar (World War II) society. The Agonshu religion was created in 1978 and was one of many that capitalized on Japanese post war reconstruction and the dissatisfaction that Japanese people felt towards religion (Meraux 1995, 1143).

The Agonshu religion was very similar to the later Aum Shinrikyo sect that Asahara would begin. The Agonshu religion had a self-professed guru, Seiyu Kiriyama who claimed that many of the benefits that individuals could claim if they became his devoted followers and paid their money. Asahara would take the teachings of yoga, self-purification, karma, psychology, neurology, and the predictions of Nostradamus and turn them into his own teachings (Lifton 2000, 19).

Asahara founded the Aum Shinsen no Kai sect in 1984 and converted his followers through his new Yoga School he had opened in Tokyo. It was through his Yoga School that he was able to spread his message and link it to the spiritual and physical healing benefits of yoga. Asahara also began to have visions during this period to reinforce his message to his disciples. These visions culminated in the Hindu deity Shiva

31

appearing before him and ordaining him. The use of a Hindu deity in a Buddhist based

religion makes sense, as Shiva is the god of yoga and is also linked to salvation after

world destruction (Lifton 2000, 19).

Sometime in the mid 1980s Asahara decided to drop the common name of Chizuo

Matsumoto and become Shoko Asahara. The new name was in line with his new image.

Asahara was connected to a field sewn with hemp, which meant connection in Buddhism

and Shoko translated to bright light. The change of name coupled with the growth of his

hair, a beard, and the adoption of the long purple robes that signify a holy man in the

Hindu religion, signified a new spiritual legitimacy. With the transformation almost

complete Asahara had his final and penultimate vision in the Himalayan Mountains,

where he claimed to achieve enlightenment in five days and which would add further

credibility amongst his followers in the new religion (Lifton 2000, 19-21).

By the end of 1986 Asahara was using his skills of manipulation, self-promotion,

and high levels of spiritual enlightenment to meet and take promotional products with

several of the world's premier spiritual leaders, including among others the Dalai Lama.

The linking of Asahara to popular figures such as the Dalai Lama added to his credibility

and his organizations standing in the religious hierarchy (Lifton 2000, 21).

Shoko Asahara and the Aum Shinrikyo

With Asahara now reshaping himself from the partially blind acupuncturist and

petty criminal to the head of a religious organization, he was also required to shape his

religion. The religious sect known as Aum Shinrikyo hailed from very humble

beginnings as a yoga center that was opened in 1984 but it did not initially have designs

on ending the world.

Asahara had begun to speak about the apocalyptic future and the role of Aum Shinrikyo as early as 1986, although it was 1989 that shaped both the group and Asahara the most. Asahara published a commentary on the book of Revelation in the New Testament, with its focus on the apocalyptic themes and one of his disciples died during a ritual (Jones 2008, 75). Previously, Asahara's religious ceremonies had been focused on his self-gratification, usually through sexual means, while forcing his followers to remain celibate and without creature comforts (Lifton 2000, 23).

After the death of the disciple Asahara demanded that his followers refer to him as Sonshi (revered master) and that killing was also a legitimate path to enlightenment. Aum Shinrikyo aggressively protected itself. It killed a member of the group who tried to leave because of the original death and burnt his body to cover the murder. After Aum Shinrikyo learnt that a television station was going to broadcast an interview with an attorney representing the murdered disciple's family in a civil lawsuit, they killed the attorney and his family (Jones 2008, 76).

Asahara and 24 of his most loyal followers ran in a local election in 1990 and were decisively defeated by all the other candidates. This embarrassed and hurt the reputation of Asahara and the sect in general. While they had already received official Japanese recognition of their religious status, along with its tax exemptions, Asahara could not understand why others would not see him as a savior in the new world order and join him (Jones 2008, 76).

After the murder of the attorney and his family and the subsequent declaration by Asahara that killing was legitimate, on the path to enlightenment, the sect began to commit many more murders, often to cover up their brazen exploitation of vulnerable

33

members. Aum is suspected of killing almost 80 different people for attempting to leave the sect or revealing insider details about it but it was not until the murder in 1995 of Kiyoshi Kariya an elderly notary public, that police suspicions were sufficiently aroused to investigate and conduct raids on Aum Shinrikyo facilities (Lifton 2001, 38-39).

While Asahara was asserting his control over the members of the sect he had been targeting certain members of Japanese society and recruiting heavily. Aum Shinrikyo looked to young people, somewhat to children, to fill out his ranks but most important were the young professionals who were well educated, Aum Shinrikyo played on their insecurities of Japanese corporate culture, and offered them a secluded world where their creativity, backed by vast financial resources could be realized (Meraux 1995, 1147-1148).

By the early 1990s Aum Shinrikyo basically consisted of three groups, the leaders who were the friends and the closest advisors to Asahara; the upper level authorities, who rejected the highly rigid conformity of Japanese society and were drawn to the resources and opportunities that Aum Shinrikyo offered them outside of the corporate world; the bottom of the pyramid were the true believers, the members who would follow Asahara anywhere and do whatever he told them (Meraux 1995, 1149).

With the sect now having independent sources of wealth through its followers, and legitimate and illegitimate business interests, it was able to focus more of its energy towards the increasingly militaristic and doomsday preaching's of its leader. By early 1990 the sect was working to develop biological weapons and attempted to release these in central Tokyo, near American Naval Stations at Yokohama and Yokos, and Narita Airport although the toxins were successfully cultivated the release mechanisms failed.

Aum Shinrikyo failed another two times to release biological agents into the population before 1995; once at the wedding of the crown prince and again in a subway station (Lifton 2001, 40).

Aum did have some success targeting individuals and small groups with toxins. It used Sarin twice to attempt to kill two rival religious leaders; VX nerve agent was used four times to target police informers and a journalist who was a critic of Aum Shinrikyo. Police were beginning to become suspicious and were now listening to families of Aum Shinrikyo members and collected soil samples that confirmed the presence of chemical toxins near one of the Aum Shinrikyo facilities as a direct result, the police inserted an undercover agent who subsequently disappeared (Lifton 2001, 39-40).

After the successful release of the Sarin gas into the Tokyo subway system Asahara ordered Aum Shinrikyo members to prevent his capture by committing acts of terror. Although never found guilty Aum Shinrikyo members were suspected of attempting to kill the Head of the National Police Agency, the Tokyo Governor and cyanide gas parcels were hidden in another subway system.

In the months after Asahara's capture on 16 May 1995 further details came to light about the group's activities. Moscow agencies confirmed that Aum scientists had approached them in the early 1990s to discuss acquiring nuclear weapons, police found pieces of missiles under an Aum Shinrikyo facility in July 1995. Thousands of rounds of ammunition, rifles, and a Soviet attack helicopter were also found in Aum Shinrikyo facilities, for the eventual preparation for Armageddon (Meraux 1995, 1153).

The Sarin gas attack assured Asahara the death penalty but has not as yet been executed (Shimbun 2012) as some of the former high level leaders have managed to evade capture or the cases against them have not been strong enough to send to trial. Aum Shinrikyo members have continued to create problems in the community, this is due to the requirements of a democratic system in dealing with an insular sub society that has a code of silence and largely does not recognize the laws or government.

On the surface Asahara and the senior members of Aum Shinrikyo created a society within Japanese culture that was based in existing religions, like Buddhism and Hinduism (Lifton 2000, 19-21). These religions promote peace, selflessness, and the ability to understand and be part of nature in a cooperative way rather that working against it. Asahara manipulated and turned the members through a series of gradual changes, until they found themselves hopelessly entangled in the crimes of Aum Shinrikyo.

Analysis

While examining Japanese democratic principles, which are contained within the Constitution of Japan, it is important to remember that Japan was transformed from 1945 to 1947 under the leadership of General MacArthur who assisted in its creation. While not word perfect, it closely mirrors the human rights based principles of other major Western powers.

Japan has experienced a growth of 18 new religions from 1800 to 1995 with a membership totaling 19 million people (Meraux 1995, 1143). This growth in religious organizations has many factors but most are linked to the pressure of Japanese society and its preoccupation with job status and earning potential, over that of spiritual enlightenment and eternal happiness (Jones 2008, 85).

There are numerous events that are linked to Asahara and Aum Shinrikyo that could have been more aggressively pursued by Japanese and even Russian authorities, which may have prevented the eventual 1995 Sarin attack. The criteria presented in table 2 will be utilized to examine if the rights guaranteed to Japanese citizens in the Constitution of Japan, possibly assisted Asahara or the wider Aum Shinrikyo to carry out their actions.

Freedom of thought, conscience, and religion, freedom of opinion and expression, and freedom of assembly and association, are the democratic principles that Asahara and Aum Shinrikyo used the most to conceal some of their actions. When Asahara published his commentary on the book of Revelation in the New Testament, it contained some of his early revelations about the possible apocalyptic future of the sect (Jones 2008, 75). Even though this was published it was not prohibited or even investigated by the authorities. It was a freedom covered by at least three parts of the Constitution of Japan. If the authorities had begun to watch the group at this stage they may have been able to prevent the escalation of the group actions into murder.

The death of a disciple during a ritual (Jones 2008, 75) and the follow up murder of a disciple who wanted to leave the sect after the death, was an escalation that may have been prevented if authorities had taken notice of the text written by Asahara and some of the radical teachings and rituals that were happening in the group. Disciples were confined in cells for long periods of time, beaten, isolated from others, and subjected to extremes in temperature (Jones 2008, 84). The missing man was eventually noticed by Japanese authorities but they were unable to overtly enter the group's facilities. The two basic rights, the right to privacy and protection of that privacy by law, and freedom of thought, conscience, and religion were protecting them.

The death of the attorney, and his family who happened to be present at the same time (Jones 2008, 76), should have triggered a larger scale response that it did, although some of the democratic freedoms discussed previously made it very hard for the authorities to be able to link the pattern together without violating those democratic rights. The group aggressively hid behind its religious rights, presumption of innocence, and the right to privacy to keep the authorities unaware of their all their illegal actions.

The suspected murder of an undercover agent was not enough for the authorities to act. If they had at this point raided the facilities, they would have been unable to use much of the evidence that they would collect, as it would have been in violation of the rights of the members and the group as whole. Even when authorities collected soil samples from around the Aum Shinrikyo facilities and found toxins that were linked to chemical and biological weapons they were unable to act, as the evidence was not absolute (Lifton 2001, 39-40).

The requirement for the law to be seen as absolute and incorruptible coupled the democratic rights that protected Aum Shinrikyo and Asahara from a proper search of investigation hampered the ability to collect evidence and enter facilities. Because the authorities were not certain that their undercover agent had been killed by Aum Shinrikyo they were unable to enter the premises to find out (Lifton 2001, 39-40).

Aum Shinrikyo was able to hide behind the veil of religion and the various democratic rights that are listed in table 2. Despite strong suspicions, the disappearance of nearly 80 people who all had Aum Shinrikyo as a common factor in their lives, the open dialogue of Asahara and his preaching's of Armageddon and the new world order, the Japanese authorities were unable to fully investigate until they had concrete evidence in 1995 (Lifton 2001, 38-39). The right to legal recourse when their rights have been violated, even if the violator was acting in an official capacity is the reason behind the lack of action by the Japanese authorities. If they were wrong or conducted a procedural error, the law and the rights surrounding it would not have allowed for that evidence to be used or produced again. This allows the suspected perpetrator to continue to act until the case against them is made.

Asahara and Aum Shinrikyo knew their rights under a democracy and used them to their advantage. By maintaining a culture of secrecy and indoctrination they were able to control information from leaving the group, which prevented the authorities from creating a case against them. The democratic rights which are protective of religions, due to previous genocides and persecution of minority groups, made Aum Shinrikyo even harder to target and prosecute and effectively shielded their actions.

Table 2.   Comparison of Democratic Principles Against the Case Study

Serial	Criteria	Aum Shinryko and Shoko Asahara	Oklahoma City and Timothy McVeigh	The London bombings and Mohammad Sidique Khan, Shehzad Tanweer, Germaine Lindsay and Hasib Hussain
1	The right to liberty and freedom of movement.	✓		
2	The right to equality before the law.	✓		
3	The right to legal recourse when their rights have been violated, even if the violator was acting in an official capacity.	✓		
4	The right to presumption of innocence until proven guilty.	✓		
5	The right to privacy and protection of that privacy by law.	✓		
6	Freedom of thought, conscience, and religion.	✓		
7	Freedom of opinion and expression.	✓		
8	Freedom of assembly and association.	✓		

Source: Created by author.

Timothy McVeigh and the Oklahoma Bombing

On 19 April 1995 at 9:02 a.m. a bomb mounted in a truck was detonated by a timer underneath the Murrah Building in Oklahoma. The blast killed 168 people and was supposed to be the start of a modern Revolutionary War, which would eventually bring about the downfall of the US Government and the African American community (Crothers 2003, 124).

Childhood and Adolescence

Timothy McVeigh was born on 23 April 1963 in upstate New York to Bill and Mildred McVeigh (Michel and Herbeck 2001, 8). By all accounts he lived a relatively normal existence as a child, going to school and not encountering any major problems at school that were noted by his teachers (Crothers 2003, 124).

McVeigh's mother Mildred chronicled her children's lives faithfully in various scrap books and journals. She took particular care to note the injuries that occurred to her children and their reactions. The injuries were not ones of neglect but rather normal childhood incidents. McVeigh's reaction was always nonchalant, even when he cut himself badly enough to reveal the bone of his skull. He never cried or yelled and would wait patiently for assistance. This is in stark contrast to incidents involving the hurting of animals. McVeigh would cry for days when he witnessed an incident involving animal cruelty and again when he begged his parents to take a wild rabbit to the vet, when it was caught by his cat (Michel and Herbeck 2001, 17).

At 10 years old McVeigh began to see the differences between the other children and himself and then between his father and himself. Timothy was bullied by an older child when his hat was stolen and then he was struck for attempting to get it back (Stout 2002, 158). McVeigh openly wept and hid in a truck and was comforted by a family friend who was watching the game. Timothy was quickly nicknamed "noodle" McVeigh by the other children do to his physique (Michel and Herbeck 2001, 18). The incident with the bully had a long lasting effect on McVeigh and fueled his hatred for bullies and any person or institution that he perceived to be picking on the weak (Michel and Herbeck 2001, 20).

Bill McVeigh was an accomplished local sportsman, especially in baseball. In his own way he attempted to involve Timothy but at the same time was pushing him away. By involving him in games of catch he was actually intimidating and reinforcing an inferiority complex in his son.

Mildred McVeigh was now working at a local travel agency. She was rekindling the love of travel she had given up to raise a family. While she still remained committed to her children, her relationship with Bill was disintegrating. Bill was working long hours at the plant and he had developed a temper, often exploding with rage at seemingly small, insignificant issues (Michel and Herbeck 2001, 20). In 1979 she told Bill that she was leaving.

The separation was amicable between Bill and Mildred McVeigh and they agreed to pursue legal separation. They decided to give the children the choice of who they wanted to be with. While the two sisters chose their mother, Timothy decided to stay with his father, out of fear of his father being alone. Mildred and Bill reconciled twice before their final split in 1984 (Michel and Herbeck 2001, 30).

Timothy was introduced to the weapons and engine mechanics by his paternal grandfather, Ed McVeigh. Ed would often take Timothy out on long walks to shoot cans or show him how to fix different objects (Michel and Herbeck 2001, 24). Ed took on the role of the father in lieu of the perpetual work schedule of Bill McVeigh, he taught Timothy all of the basic domestic tasks and stoked his interests in weapons and shooting (Currie 2002, 58).

By the age of 17 Timothy was living alone with his father. Bill had changed his shifts to work nights, in an attempt to bond with his son but the years of absent parenting had already ensured the damage was done. Timothy was becoming more isolated and goal orientated. His desire for computers and the internet led him to hack several computer networks. Long before computers were accessible to the main population, he even managed to hack into the White Sands Missile Defense Range in New Mexico. A practical joke by another hacker, led Timothy to believe that he was being pursued by the government and he would not leave his house until the hacker told him of the practical joke (Michel and Herbeck 2001, 32).

Timothy McVeigh graduated in 1986 and attained a scholarship award from New York State. Timothy started a period a self-reflection after graduation and began to realize the threat of a nuclear winter and that he would need survival and weapon skills. Timothy began to research the Second Amendment. He was soon convinced by his father to enroll in a small local college to study computers. He was dismayed when he learnt the school would require him to do a number of other courses as well. He soon dropped out to concentrate on working at Burger King and on his pursuit of survival skills and weapons (Michel and Herbeck 2001, 38-39).

It was while Timothy was reading that two main works stood out to him, the first *To ride, Shoot Straight and Speak the Truth*, by Jeff Cooper (a renowned ex-military survivalist and weapons expert) spoke to him about a warrior attitude to life in general, to be prepared and aware. The second text was *'The Turner Diaries*, by American Nazi Party Official William L. Pierce. This text discusses the government taking away the civil rights of citizens (mainly the Second Amendment) and a young man resisting by making a truck bomb and blowing up the Federal Bureau of Investigation Headquarters in

Washington. As Hitler did, the text also espouses similar hate messages against those of Jewish or African decent (Stout 2002, 158).

Through his reading, grandfather, and lessons of his upbringing his survivalist and weapons centric mentality reached fruition in his adolescent brain. Timothy decided to start his own weapon collection. To finance this he became an armed security guard and in the fall of 1987 became a guard for Burke Armored Car Service. This job would take him from his predominately white rural neighborhood, to the city of Buffalo with its ghettos and mixed races (Michel and Herbeck 2001, 43).

While working as a security guard, Timothy witnessed the racist taunts of his co-workers, "There they are-the porch monkeys" (Michel and Herbeck 2001, 43) and other such racial slurs. Timothy worked in a poor, mainly African American part of Buffalo, so his perception was based on observing the lines of African Americans lining up to cash their checks. This attitude was only to harden in the years ahead.

While the picture of Timothy McVeigh seems to be relatively normal, his own memory details his upbringing as less than happy. "I have very few memories . . . of interaction with my parents," he stated. "I was often by myself or with neighbors." (Michel and Herbeck 2001, 7). In May 1988, at 20 years old Timothy McVeigh joined the Army in search of adventure and meaning in his life (Currie 2002, 58).

The Army

The beginning of Army life was the normal rite of passage that so many before McVeigh had been through. The yelling, setting of impossible goals, and belittling of the new recruits. McVeigh soon caught onto the Army way of teaching and enjoyed the cadences that called for killing or committing violent sex acts with women (Stout 2002, 159).

McVeigh was randomly selected to become part of an Army Trail Program named COHORT, which was an acronym for Cohesion, Operational Readiness and Training. The aim of the program was to develop permanent small teams in basic training and keep them going through the first three years of Army life, to maintain retention and a shared sense of purpose amongst the new recruits (Michel and Herbeck 2001, 53-54).

While at Fort Benning, McVeigh met with Terry Lynn Nichols and Michael J. Fortier who shared some of his more radical racial views. The three became his best friends and future partners in the events of 19 April 1995 (Crothers 2003, 124). Nichols, a fellow recruit was also a squad leader and according to other recruits at the time, was a charismatic leader and powerful influence on McVeigh (Michel and Herbeck 2001, 56).

Basic training was a success for McVeigh. He finished with the top test score for an Infantry trainee (Michel and Herbeck 2001, 58), had filled out his scrawny frame with muscle and found a career that he loved. He was moved to Fort Riley, Kansas to complete advanced Infantry training with Nichols in August 1988.

At Fort Riley, McVeigh, Nichols, and Fortier were assigned to the same squad but Nichols left the Army in spring 1989 due to family issues at home, which pushed McVeigh and Fortier together (Michel and Herbeck 2001, 59). The comparatively relaxed time schedule at Fort Riley allowed McVeigh to continue reading. His attention had now turned to gun laws, the Revolutionary War, and a conspiracy between the UN and the US to restrict civil liberties in the US. It was also during this time that McVeigh gave Fortier a copy of *The Turner Diaries* to read (Crothers 2003, 126).

McVeigh also gave two other soldiers in his unit copies of the *The Turner Diaries*, Sergeants Rodriguez and Warnement. Both of these soldiers gave McVeigh advice to not keep the text on Army property and to stop handing it out as it went against Army regulations. McVeigh did not listen and continued to hand the material out to his friends (Michel and Herbeck 2001, 64).

McVeigh was allocated as a Bradley Infantry Fighting Vehicle gunner and was so proficient that his was selected to be the Division Display Vehicle for General Officer and politician visits. McVeigh was so happy with his career that he re-signed for another four years in September 1990 (Michel and Herbeck 2001, 64).

McVeigh became more obsessed with right wing racist and anti-government propaganda throughout his time in the Army. Although there is no evidence to suggest the Army contributed to this, his friendship with Fortier did help to facilitate it. McVeigh also grew lonely after his friend, Nichols, left the Army, which left him with more time on his hands. McVeigh chose to spend some of this time beginning his training regime for Special Forces selection but was interrupted by the first Gulf War (Crothers 2003, 127).

McVeigh deployed to the Persian Gulf and spent much of his first few months waiting for the ground attack order to be promulgated. McVeigh was nervous on the morning of the ground war commencement. He was expecting heavy resistance from the Iraqi Army. When he finally gained contact with them, he found them to be bedraggled and scared from the Air Campaign; nothing like the blood crazed soldiers he was told to expect (Michel and Herbeck 2001, 73-74).

He also began to despise the Army system, as he felt that his Commanding Officer did not know as much as he did, yet he was still required to follow orders unquestioningly. McVeigh was awarded an Army Commendation Medal for destroying an Iraqi machine gun nest but he was upset at the taking of human life (Michel and Herbeck 2001, 75).

McVeigh was bothered by the war in many ways, being part of a UN Force, the sight of hundreds of dead Iraqis, the lack of resistance, his own killing of human beings, and the length of the war. What upset him the most was detailed in his later allegations of some US soldiers killing surrendering Iraqi forces (Michel and Herbeck 2001, 80).

McVeigh was recalled to attend the Special Forces selection test. He failed. The war had ruined McVeigh's preparation time. He was underprepared to undergo such a grueling course (Currie 2002, 61).

McVeigh returned to Fort Riley a different person. He still excelled at Army tasks but showed bitterness and anger towards others and the tasks, and spent much of his time in isolation. McVeigh also noticed a change in the Army, an African American Private threatened a fellow soldier with a gun; some African American soldiers walked around the base wearing black power shirts and addressed McVeigh as "Sarge". McVeigh could barely tolerate these African American soldiers, who flouted the rules and had it easier than the Caucasian soldier (Michel and Herbeck 2001, 87).

McVeigh insisted that he was not a racist and that he had several African American soldiers as friends and that he also hated some Caucasian soldiers. Irrespective of McVeigh's protests he was labeled a racist on the base by some and did admit to calling some African American soldiers "niggers" (Michel and Herbeck 2001, 88).

47

McVeigh was still an exemplary soldier. He was admired for his skills and professionalism by senior officers and looked every bit like the warrior soldier. McVeigh was requested to become the Battalion Commander's gunner on his vehicle. McVeigh was flattered but was also aware that he would be required to perform other duties with officers and enlisted that he did not want to do. To the surprise of everyone, McVeigh not only turned down the offer but also quit the Army. By the end of 1991 he was driving home to his father (Michel and Herbeck 2001, 90-91).

Post Army

McVeigh thought that his military career would afford him a higher level of respect in the community but was mistaken. He found it hard to get a job and ended up working in security again. He had to supplement his income by joining the National Guard (Michel and Herbeck 2001, 96).

As McVeigh became disenchanted, he became angry. He had two altercations at his security job with a co-worker and a manager and wrote a letter to the Lockport *Union Sun & Journal*, complaining about prisons, crime, and the dissolution of the American dream. He also wrote to Representative John LaFalce complaining about an incident in which he perceived a citizen's Second Amendment rights were infringed upon (Michel and Herbeck 2001, 98-99).

In the latter stages of 1992 McVeigh quit his job and moved to Michigan to join with Nichols. It was while he was staying with Nichols that he watched the events unfold on Ruby Ridge. Again in February1993 McVeigh watched with anger at the first raid of the Brach Davidian Sect in Waco, Texas. McVeigh actually drove to the site and attempted entry. His treatment by the guards reinforced his perception of the government

48

impinging his basic rights. McVeigh sold bumper stickers at the rest area near the compound and was interviewed. The interview indicated that his views had hardened and he was willing to let a wider group know it (Michel and Herbeck 2001, 118-120).

McVeigh spent time at gun shows, selling books and right wing literature. He found many people sympathetic to his views at these shows and spent a great deal of time listening to anti-government talk shows at night. During these travels he met numerous right wing people and listened to their ideas. By the end of the 1993 Tulsa gun show, McVeigh was discussing the "New World Order" which postulated a world take over by the UN and the creation of a single ruling government over mankind (Michel and Herbeck 2001, 126).

McVeigh decided that he would reunite with Terry Nichols on his farm and on 19 April 1993 watched the final raid occur in Waco. McVeigh and Nichols agreed a government conspiracy occurred at Waco, that the Alcohol, Tobacco and Firearms acted illegally by not having warrants, and the fire was set on purpose (Michel and Herbeck 2001, 136).

McVeigh travelled back to see Fortier in Arizona where he attended more gun shows, selling flare guns that he claimed could be used to shoot down helicopters, even telling an undercover detective at the Phoenix gun show that they could have been used in Waco to defend the sect. Nothing came of the incident which steeled McVeigh into thinking he was right (Michel and Herbeck 2001, 98-99).

In 1994, several events suddenly occurred in McVeigh's life; his grandfather, a pivotal part of his life, became terminally ill. McVeigh decided that he was going to destroy a Federal building and he wanted Fortier to assist him. Fortier initially refused to help him but McVeigh was convinced he would eventually assist. Nichols and McVeigh had stolen explosives from a quarry and purchased four thousand pounds of ammonium nitrate. He would eventually make eight purchases all together (Michel and Herbeck 2001, 98-99). McVeigh assembled the rest of his bomb and attacked on 19 April 1995.

Analysis

There are several events in the life of McVeigh which stand out as critical events, which if pursued by authorities may have stopped the eventual attack. By examining the criteria presented in the table at the end of chapter 3 against the events in the case study, a hypothesis will be drawn; if democracy shielded McVeigh's actions, or if other, external factors not related to democracy were primarily responsible.

The first event is the text *The Turner Diaries*, a white supremacist text which alludes to an African American takeover of American society and "patriotic" whites uniting the white population and fighting back. This text is protected by freedom of thought, conscience, and religion, and freedom of opinion and expression. *The Turner Diaries* is clearly protected from any adverse action on the grounds that it would be discrimination and it can be argued that if McVeigh wished to, he had every right to read whatever he wanted.

It is the unknown psychological effect of literature like the *The Turner Diaries* that when coupled with a singular perspective of an issue (in this case an entire race of people) can cause the polarizing of a particular point of thought or thought pattern. McVeigh had not had good experiences with African American people in his life. His experiences as a security guard, where the majority of neighborhoods he transited through were ethnically African American and poverty stricken, coupled with the racist

50

views of his co-workers began to plant a negative stereotype (Michel and Herbeck 2001, 43). This stereotype was then reinforced by *The Turner Diaries* and the alleged incidents. After his return from the Gulf War he was again negatively influenced by the actions of a very small minority of African American soldiers at Fort Riley (Michel and Herbeck 2001, 87).

The US Army also has a portion of the blame as well. When McVeigh gave two senior members of his unit, Sergeants Rodriguez and Warnement the text, they warned him that it was an offense to distribute this type of material on military property but did not report him (Michel and Herbeck 2001, 64). Also by only judging McVeigh on his skill as a Bradley Infantry Fighting Vehicle gunner and not as a whole soldier he was elevated to a position of power that was not commensurate with his rank, age, or experience. While McVeigh was winning Divisional Level competitions and being presented to politicians and senior Army leadership figures, he may have been aware that not only was the Army failing to enforce their own regulations but they were doing so knowingly and then were rewarding him (Michel and Herbeck 2001, 90-91).

The very existence of the *The Turner Diaries* while not illegal did provide a supposedly legitimate outside negative reinforcement of McVeigh's immature and narrow view of African Americans in general. *The Turner Diaries*, while not responsible for the Oklahoma attack, did inspire and add a sense of legitimacy to the views that McVeigh had formulated.

The right to privacy and protection of that privacy by law; freedom of thought, conscience, and religion, and freedom of opinion and expression, were all vulnerabilities that were exploited by McVeigh when he wrote two letters; one to the Lockport *Union*

51

Sun & Journal and one to Representative John LaFalce. Both letters gave indirect insights into the thoughts and direction that McVeigh was heading. His argument to the Lockport *Union Sun & Journal* which centered on what he thought was the end of the "American dream" and the dissolution of constitutional rights, in general displays an eerie echo of the conditions listed in *The Turner Diaries*. The second letter to Representative John LaFalce is openly hostile to what McVeigh perceived to be the erosion of the Second Amendment. While it did not contain a specific threat, its intention, coupled with the first letter, shows a clear line of thought (Michel and Herbeck 2001, 98-99).

The rights under a democracy to write these letters and to have your voice heard are the keystones to a governmental system that includes a participative population. McVeigh was in essence expressing his opinions in a manner that was allowed and enshrined in law. In retrospect perhaps these messages should have been followed up by a local or federal body as a possible indication of an extremist.

The right to privacy and protection of that privacy by law; freedom of thought, conscience, and religion, and freedom of opinion and expression also relate to the radio shows and eventual racist literature that McVeigh was distributing at various gun shows (Michel and Herbeck 2001, 126). McVeigh was even spoken to by an undercover police officer at these shows and admitted to being able to sell weapons that could be used against Federal agencies. McVeigh was also selling racist material and literature at these shows and neither the organizers, patrons, nor other participants stopped him. This could be because they felt that it was within the rights of an individual to express their views and that others can either ignore or participate as they wish but that this is a personal decision. McVeigh did fall in with a group of people that listened to anti-government talk shows at night. These talk shows espoused the disintegration of the government by the people, asserting that minority rights were growing against the majority's interests, and described the erosion of individual and collective rights as enshrined under a democracy (Michel and Herbeck 2001, 126).

The talk shows' right to criticize the democratic government and processes which safeguards its rights to conduct the criticism was a premise that was lost to McVeigh. McVeigh was a ripe target to be molded by propaganda and messaging from the various right wing groups that existed around him. The talk shows added to the sense of impending doom that McVeigh had in the end, of the democratic American society that he loved.

There is a problem that occurs at this juncture in the analysis. It could be argued that if democracy was working and the police officer acted correctly, then McVeigh would have been arrested for the alleged threat against a Federal agency, specifically the Alcohol, Tobacco and Firearms. As it is hypothetical to assume that an arrest here would have stopped a later incident, the thesis will continue with the facts only, acknowledging that the incident took place but not conducting any other analysis on this subject.

The Ruby Ridge and Waco incidents ironically angered McVeigh because he believed that he Federal agents were not adhering to any of the ideals of democracy. Some of the elements of democracy that had up until now been shielding McVeigh from the authorities and from general notice were now perceived by him to being denied to the inhabitants of those areas. McVeigh decided to travel to Waco and handed out bumper stickers and was even interviewed by a local television reporter (Michel and Herbeck

2001, 118-120). His views were more intense than the views that he espoused in his earlier two letters that he wrote.

All of the elements of democracy were present in the McVeigh case. All of them effectively shielded him from view which consequently allowed him to carry out his final act of terror. On several occasions McVeigh publicly displayed his opinions and each time he was allowed to do so, as such the severity and clarity of his eventual message became stronger, from his passive observations of the other workers in the security company calling African Americans "porch monkeys" (Michel and Herbeck 2001, 43) to him openly selling racist literature in front of law enforcement official's (Michel and Herbeck 2001, 126) and broadcasting his anti-government views at the Waco siege on public television (Michel and Herbeck 2001, 118-120).

Table 3.   Comparison of Democratic Principles Against the Case Study

Serial	Criteria	Aum Shinryko and Shoko Asahara	Oklahoma City and Timothy McVeigh	The London bombings and Mohammad Sidique Khan, Shehzad Tanweer, Germaine Lindsay and Hasib Hussain
1	The right to liberty and freedom of movement.	✓	✓	
2	The right to equality before the law.	✓	✓	
3	The right to legal recourse when their rights have been violated, even if the violator was acting in an official capacity.	✓	✓	
4	The right to presumption of innocence until proven guilty.	✓	✓	
5	The right to privacy and protection of that privacy by law.	✓	✓	
6	Freedom of thought, conscience, and religion.	✓	✓	
7	Freedom of opinion and expression.	✓	✓	
8	Freedom of assembly and association.	✓	✓	

Source: Created by author.

The 2005 London Bombings and Mohammad Sidique Khan, Shehzad Tanweer, Germaine Lindsay, and Hasib Hussain

On 7 July 2005, at 0850 Shehzad Tanweer, a British National of Pakistani heritage blew himself up on the eastbound Circle Line Train, killing 8 people including Tanweer, and injuring 171 others. Simultaneously at the Edgware Road Line and Piccadilly Line, Mohammad Sidique Khan and Germaine Lindsay detonated their suicide devices killing 34 people and injuring 504 between them. The fourth suicide bomber,

Hasib Hussain boards the Number 30 Bus, which is unusually crowded due to the now closed underground and sits on the top deck, detonating his device at 0947 killing 14 people and injuring 110 (House of Commons 2006, 5-6).

The Terrorists

The four men who committed the act of terrorism were not extraordinary; they were in fact ordinary and did not have any significant parts of their background that made them stand out amongst others in the communities that they resided in. Khan, Tanweer and Hussain will be analyzed first, due to their distinct commonalties of heritage, upbringing, and nationality. Lindsay will be considered last due to some of the distinct differences of his case.

The area in which Khan, Tanweer and Hussain grew up is a reasonably generic part of the UK. It is dominated by residential dwellings which are back to back terraced houses with a high level of ethnic diversity many of the buildings are in a poor condition. The businesses in the area reflect the ethnic and religious identification of the residents. There are several mosques, a modern community center, sporting facilities (football and cricket), and a closed (was open on 7 July 2005) Islamic bookshop. The area is regarded as impoverished by UK standards with the average income being lower than the median and "over 10,000 of the 16,300 residents have living standards that are amongst the worst 3% nationally" (House of Commons 2006, 13). Although the area itself was poor Khan, Tanweer and Hussain were not poor compared to others in the area, in fact Tanweer's father was a successful local businessman (House of Commons 2006, 13).

Mohammad Sidique Khan

Mohammad Sidique Khan was born on 20 October 1974 and raised in a suburb called Beeston in Leeds. His parents were from Pakistan, having immigrated to the UK. Khan was educated locally in the school system and was remembered as a quiet, intelligent boy who was not a trouble maker but was sometimes bullied (House of Commons 2006, 13).

In September 1996 Khan attended the Leeds Metropolitan University to study business and achieved a 2.2 (lower second class honors which is approximately equal to a US Grade Point Average of 3.00 to 3.32). He also seemed to develop his later passion for helping disadvantaged young people, as he began to help with various community youth organizations. While at the University he met the woman who was to become his future wife Hasina, a British Muslim of Indian origin, who was a social activist for women's rights (Ranstorp 2010, 103). The marriage to his wife on 22 October 2001 caused some minor problems between the newlywed pair and their parents as the marriage was not officially arranged by the parents. It appears that this was only a brief concern as both sets of parents eventually gave their consent to the union (House of Commons 2006, 13).

In 1997 Khan took part in a demonstration against the Leeds City Council and their decision to build houses on a location that had previously been allocated to the building of a new community center. The demonstration was organized by the Kashmiri Welfare Association and Khan gave an interview to the *Yorkshire Evening Post* where he advocated the need to enhance youth services in the area. Besides the actual bombings, Khan was also interviewed by *The Times* in 2002 about the educational achievements of his school. He was enthusiastic about the gains made by the teachers and students but critical of the local government for not providing enough resources (Ranstorp 2010, 103).

Khan remained firm in his commitment to the local community, utilizing his religious connections at the Hardy Street Mosque and through his local connections he secured a local government grant, to establish the first of two gymnasiums in February 2000. The gym was aligned underneath the Kashmiri Welfare Association and had the goal of keeping disaffected youth off the streets by involving them in weightlifting (Tumelty 2005).

Between 2001 and 2004 Khan worked for the Hillside Primary School as a learning mentor, which required him to work closely with teachers to help students who were experiencing learning difficulties (Ranstorp 2010, 103). Khan was a dedicated member of the faculty who took great pride in his work. After the bombing, the head teacher at the school stated "Sidique was a real asset to the school and always showed one hundred percent commitment" (Rai 2006, 25). The majority of his worked focused on the children of recently arrived immigrants to the country, assisting them to assimilate and overcome any learning barriers (Ranstorp 2010, 103).

It is possible that Khan made several trips to the Afghanistan and Pakistan regions since the mid 1990s, although there is no distinct proof of this occurring. Khan did visit Pakistan at some point in 2003 for two weeks and resided close to the border with Afghanistan. Khan's activities during that time are unknown but given the area that he visited it is highly probable that there would have been some impact, motivational or psychological on him (House of Commons 2006, 20).

Khan was extremely busy in all parts of his life throughout 2004. On 14 May he welcomed his first daughter, Maryam into the world (Rai 2006, 26). Khan also decided to set up his second gymnasium, this time in conjunction with the Hamara Centre Charitable Foundation which would also focus on local youth. The Lodge Lane, as it was known, would become central to the later training of the four terrorists as it is alleged they used the gymnasium when it was closed for renovations (Tumelty 2005). Khan also decided to move his family at the end of 2004 to a new house in Dewsbury, which is about 10 miles south of Leeds, he rented from the local council and began to redecorate. With the eventual terrorist act only six months away his neighbors remained clueless "He didn't seem like an extremist. He was not one to talk about religion. He was generally a very nice bloke" (Rai 2006, 27). There are two parts to 2004 that stand out as abnormal when compared to the rest of Khan's life. First, he began to have poor attendance and unexplained absences at work, this culminated in the period 20 September to 19 November 2004, during which he claimed he was sick. Subsequently he was fired from the school (House of Commons 2006, 15). Secondly he was asked to leave the Hardy Street Mosque for allegedly preaching extremist ideology to other members (Tumelty 2005).

Khan visited Pakistan with Tanweer from 19 November 2004 to 9 February 2005. It is unclear as to what activities the pair conducted when they arrived but their original excuse to go was to further their knowledge and study of Islam. Khan and Tanweer split up and the whereabouts of Khan during this time is unknown. After a week he returned and took Tanweer for another two weeks to another undisclosed location. There is no evidence to suggest that Khan engaged in training or fighting in Pakistan or Afghanistan but it is likely that he made his final video here and met with senior Al Qaeda figures (House of Commons 2006, 19).

Khan and Tanweer were linked to an investigation into an alleged terrorist cell in March 2004. The operation, codenamed Operation Crevice was tracking a group of young, Muslim British-Pakistanis that were suspected of attempting to plan a terrorist bombing of London. Khan and Tanweer were only identified as possible associates that appeared on the fringe of the investigation and not as suspects. As a result there were no further investigations into either of the men (Ranstorp 2010, 104).

The community around Khan remember him as a dedicated educator and champion of immigrants in his local community. However, with hindsight many now remember some subtle changes in his attitude and demeanor in the months that led up to the attack. Hearsay evidence alleges that Khan, Tanweer, and Lindsay had attended some prayer meetings with radical Sheiks in London, including Abu Hamza and that they had been seen watching extremist videos and reading extremist literature, in the local Islamic book shop (Randstorp 2010, 104). Besides the actual act of terror the only evidence firmly linking Khan to extremism is his video explanation made before the attack and his will. In the video Khan links his perception of injustices that have been performed by the West against Islam and that the Quran allows for retribution through violence. In his will he focused on the importance of martyrdom and the supreme act of religious commitment (House of Commons 2006, 19).

Shehzad Tanweer

The story of Shehzad Tanweer is closely entwined with Kahn as they spent a good deal of time together and spent a lot of time travelling. Tanweer was a British born citizen to Pakistani immigrant parents. He was born into and stayed in the same area as Kahn and they grew up together, although they were not close friends until after secondary school. Tanweer's parents originally came to England to further their trade skills but ended up becoming permanent citizens when they opened a series of stores, their family is considered to be in the middle upper class of English society (Rai 2006, 31).

Tanweer was obsessed with sports, especially cricket which he played and excelled at. Tanweer often discussed his dream of playing professional cricket for England and went onto study Sports Science at Leeds Metropolitan University. There is no evidence to suggest that he was exposed to any racism, bullying, or that he experienced any social difficulties (Randstorp 2010, 104).

Tanweer was not shy about his family's wealth or his talent. He dressed in fashionable clothes and bought only the best sportswear and he owned his own car. Like Kahn, Tanweer was also active in the community; he volunteered his time with local sporting clubs to help in the junior competitions and also became involved with the Jamaat al-Dawa wa-al-Tabligh missionary movement to further his social work (Randstorp 2010, 105).

Tanweer did take religion seriously since he was a small child; a family friend remarked that "he's a very religious lad, but a lot of his friends are white. He never put a white man down. He called me his uncle Neil. I can't believe he could be a religious fanatic" (Rai 2006, 32). His friends at school noticed a change in Tanweer when he turned 16 and he became more religiously observant and then again in 2002 when he left his university course early for an unknown reason. Tanweer spent his newly found spare time conducting physical training and studying religion. There were no outward signs of extremism, just devotion to Islam (House of Commons 2006, 15)

At some point after the attacks on the 11 September 2001, Tanweer rekindled his relationship with Kahn. Tanweer began to train and frequent the gymnasiums and stopped maintaining contact with his other friends that he had developed through sports and school. He and Khan would often train together or go into London to attend the Finsbury Park Mosque and listen to Hamza. The other terrorists, Hussein and Lindsay would sometimes join them but it was obvious that Khan and Tanweer had formed a special bond (Randstorp 2010, 105).

Tanweer went to Pakistan with Khan in November 2004 and flew to the Pakistani city of Karahi. Tanweer had told his family that he was going to learn the Quran by heart and to find a good religious school (Tumelty 2005). Upon arrival in Pakistan Khan left him and Tanweer headed to his ancestral home of Faisalbad where he studied and prayed, only leaving for a two week period to go with Khan to an undisclosed location (Randstorp 2010, 105).

Tanweer's relatives in Pakistan noticed the first major changes in his behavior; they commented that he suddenly became much more religious, praying five times a day and growing his beard. He also became a vocal critic of British politics and his countries role in the Afghanistan and Iraq conflicts and openly praised bin Laden and his assault on America. Tanweer also expressed immense solidarity for the Muslim fighters in the disputed Kashmir region and used some of the money that his father sent him, to buy winter coats for the fighters (Randstorp 2010, 105).

Tanweer left a video message, delivered to Al Jazeera from the Al Shabab terror network. In the video Tanweer echoed some of the extremist leaders, in particular Ayman al-Zawahiri. Tanweer spoke of the suffering of Muslims at the hands of the UK Government and of the supposed genocide of Muslims in Fallujah (Randstorp 2010, 106).

Taweer is remembered as an excellent athlete and sportsman who loved his family and his life. The day prior to the bombing Tanweer had gone to the local park and played sport, laughing and joking with friends. These same friends describe him as a person who "seemed to enjoy everything British and Western, and had the means to do so" (Rai 2006, 32).

Hasib Hussain

The most unremarkable and least written about member is Hasib Hussain. Hussain grew up in the same area as both Tanweer and Khan and seems to have led a very normal life, as a member of that community, leaving school at the age of 16 with no qualifications and no real future (Kirby 2007, 417).

Hussain was involved in some illicit drug use when he was a teenager and came to the attention of the police for marijuana use and fighting with some other white teenagers in the area (Tumelty, 2005). Hussain was a keen sportsman and followed both cricket and football, although he was bullied by other students at his school for being slightly overweight (Kirby 2007, 417). His parents sent him to Pakistan to try and get him to accept and follow the traditional Islamic life and cease his drug use, although while all parties accept that he did undertake a four week trip to Pakistan in 2002, his family claims it was for a wedding and not for any religious reasons (Rai 2006, 46).

In 2003, Hussain experienced a number of setbacks in his personal life which may have contributed to his new persona, which was one of a devout student of Islam. This also coincided with his return from Pakistan. What is known though is that he was withdrawn from all of his classes except for one by his school after a physical altercation with some girls, his football team closed, and he changed into a very religious young man in a very short period of time (Rai 2007, 46-47).

Hussain's elder brother and father did not like the changes that took place in Hussain prior to the attack. They spoke at length about the people he was now associating with (Khan) and the changes that had occurred. They decided that the worst that could happen was that he would be praying a lot more and decided to let Hussain do what he wanted to (Randstorp 2010, 107).

It is unknown if Hussain attended some of the lectures given by the more radical clerics such as Hamza but he did attend the same gym, mosque, and bookshop as the other members of the cell (Randstorp 2010, 107).

Germaine Lindsay

Germaine Lindsay, also known as Abdullah Shaheed Jamal is perhaps the strangest member of the group. Lindsay was born in Jamaica to his then teenage mother before moving to the UK in 1986 when he was just one year old. Lindsay lived in the town of Huddlesfield, which is close to Leeds and it is alleged that his stepfather treated him very harshly but left in 1990 (House of Commons 2006, 17).

At some time post 1990 his mother met and began a relationship with a Muslim man who stayed with the family until 2000. Lindsay grew close to his new stepfather and spent a lot of time with him. His mother converted to Islam after the relationship ended in

2000 and Lindsay followed in 2001 and took the name Abdullah Shaheed Jamal (Tumelty 2005).

Lindsay did well at school and was an intelligent student. He was also good at sports, in particular football and boxing, and spent a lot of time in the gym practicing. His fellow students and teachers noticed a change in him after the he converted to Islam at the age of 15. He immediately stopped smoking, listening to non-Islamic music and playing football and began to listen to tapes of Islamic preachers on his personal stereo in class (Rai 2007, 37). Lindsay's teachers also began to notice a difference in him. He began to associate with known troublemakers and was disciplined for handing out pro Al Qaeda literature (House of Commons 2006, 18).

In 2002 Lindsay's mother met another man and moved to the US to be with him. Lindsay was left behind in England and this event was very destabilizing for him, he left school and when he was not receiving government welfare, worked selling mobile phones and Islamic literature. Lindsay did continue to train and attended many gyms, including the ones which Khan had set up; it is likely that this is where the two first met (House of Commons 2006, 18).

Lindsay married a convert to Islam that he met in an internet chat room and then again at an anti-Iraq War rally. He moved twice before the bombings and his first child was born on 11 April 2004. Prior to the bombings Lindsay's brother-in-law managed to secure him some temporary work (Randstorp 2010, 108).

Lindsay did go in search of religious fulfillment several times after he converted to Islam. He is linked to the radical preacher Hamza, along with Khan and Tanweer and is also linked to another extremist preacher Abdallah al Faisal (also of Jamaican origin)

65

who is currently in jail for incitement to murder, incitement to racial hatred, distributing material of a racial hatred nature, and soliciting murder (House of Commons 2006, 18).

Lindsay was very similar to Hussain in the way in which he is remembered by the community around him. The members of the mosque that he frequented remember him an intelligent, dedicated pupil of Islam. His wife remembers him as a kind loving husband who changed after their marriage. She summed up his radicalization by saying that "he was an innocent, naive, and simple man. I suppose he must have been the ideal candidate" (Rai 2006, 39).

Analysis

The democratic principles that exist in the UK are very similar to those that exist in the US and Japan. Therefore, fair comparison can be made against the previous two countries and terrorist acts.

Khan, Tanweer, Hussain, and Lindsay definitely had the right to freedom of movement and liberty in their case study. When Khan and Tanweer were allowed to travel to Pakistan for personal reasons and return without question they exercised this right, even when Khan travelled to the remote tribal regions for unexplained reasons in the late 1990s he was not stopped or even questioned because of this democratic principle (House of Commons 2006, 20).

The person who exercised this right the most was probably Lindsay. The movement of his family to the UK from Jamaica and then the unrestricted movement of his mother to the US shows a commonality between the two countries and the existence of this right. Even after being identified as attending extremist preachings, antiwar rallies, and handing out pro Al Qaeda material both Khan and Lindsay were not monitored or restricted in their movements (House of Commons 2006, 18).

Both Hussain and Lindsay experienced the right of equality before the law during their adolescent years. For Hussain his casual drug use and fighting with other young men was dealt with fairly by the police, without bias or prejudice (Tumelty 2005). Lindsay also was dealt with fairly when he handed out pro Al Qaeda literature (House of Commons 2006, 18).

It can also be argued that the two radical preachers listed in the case study, Hamza and al Faisal have also experienced equality before the law. While only al Faisal is currently in jail he was allowed a great deal of latitude before he was tried and convicted in a court of law. Any previous suspicions and biases were not allowed in the court and therefore al Faisal was only convicted on the facts, rather than what people suspected him of committing (House of Commons 2006, 18).

The right to legal recourse when their rights have been violated, even if the violator was acting in an official capacity is an interesting right that all four of the terrorists exercised. With hindsight there are many occasions when authorities could have moved in and used the trips to Pakistan, the concerns of teachers and friends about changes in behavior, and the attendance at radical preaching's as excuses. It was due to a self-policing system, with well enshrined rights that prevented them from doing so and this right in particular that forces authorities to get the most reliable and proven sources, before being allowed to apprehend a suspect.

All four of the suspects used the right to privacy and protection of that privacy by law to their advantage. Khan and Tanweer used the ability to travel to Pakistan and not have to tell their home country the details of what they did while they were overseas and the UK was prohibited from tracking them, as they had no suspicion of any wrongdoing (House of Commons 2006, 19). Three of the members attended the radical preachings of Hamza, their privacy was respected by the authorities, and they were not tracked or infiltrated after attending (House of Commons 2006, 18). Khan's purchase and use of the gym and the Islamic bookstore also did not cause any issues, although given the groups past activities and in some cases open dissidence against the society in which they lived, they were allowed continuous privilege of this right. Even after the event, the families of the terrorists used their right to privacy to stop the media from interviewing or harassing them and to only issue statements of denial or regret (Rai 2006, 29-39).

The final three rights, freedom of thought, conscience, and religion, freedom of opinion and expression, and freedom of assembly and association will be discussed together as they are largely intertwined. It is obvious that all were allowed the freedom of thought, conscience and religion, they all began as very moderate Muslims and even a Christian before becoming extremists and then radicalized. There were allowed to practice their religion without fear and without prejudice in their communities.

Hussain and Lindsay were allowed to express their opinions in government run schools. Although they were disciplined for spreading hate amongst the school population, they were not adversely disadvantaged or told they were to cease believing in a certain religion (House of Commons 2006, 18). Khan was asked to leave the local mosque which he utilized for prayer because of his views but he was not persecuted or reported to the authorities for doing so (Tumelty 2005).

Khan, Tanweer and Lindsay were all allowed the right to assembly and freedom of association. For Khan and Lindsay they attended several public actions, in Khans' case not motivated by religion but for Lindsay it was motivated by the Iraq War. For all of the members, less Hussain, they were allowed to attend the radical lectures then associate with others, like Hussain to spread the words of the preachers. The clearest representation of the respect the authorities had for this right was when Khan and Tanweer were mentioned in Operation Crevice. The authorities did not pursue them at all as they were merely associates and not involved in the actual incident (Randstorp 2010, 103-108).

It is unclear if Khan, Tanweer, Hussain, and Lindsay actively used their rights under a democracy to allow them to commit their act of terror. It is clear though that many markers, clearly visible after the fact, were shielded from the eyes of authorities. Trips to the tribal regions of Pakistan, radical changes in behavior, being asked to leave their previous places of worship, distributing support for a banned organization, and association with known radicals are just a few of the markers that were present. It is clear that the democratic rights obscured the authorities' view of the complete picture and prohibited any early action to thwart their final action.

Table 4.   Comparison of Democratic Principles Against the Case Study

Serial	Criteria	Aum Shinryko and Shoko Asahara	Oklahoma City and Timothy McVeigh	The London bombings and Mohammad Sidique Khan, Shehzad Tanweer, Germaine Lindsay and Hasib Hussain
1	The right to liberty and freedom of movement.	✔	✔	✔
2	The right to equality before the law.	✔	✔	✔
3	The right to legal recourse when their rights have been violated, even if the violator was acting in an official capacity.	✔	✔	✔
4	The right to presumption of innocence until proven guilty.	✔	✔	NA (all suspects died before trial)
5	The right to privacy and protection of that privacy by law.	✔	✔	✔
6	Freedom of thought, conscience, and religion.	✔	✔	✔
7	Freedom of opinion and expression.	✔	✔	✔
8	Freedom of assembly and association.	✔	✔	✔

Source: Created by author.

CHAPTER 5

CONCLUSIONS AND RECOMMENDATIONS

Summary

There are three distinct themes which are prevalent throughout the thesis: bullying, a perceived or actual failure in the administrative architecture of the state, and the use of violence to solve problems. Each one will be discussed in detail.

Bullying

McVeigh was a classic example of a bullied child; he was bullied by the children around him due to his physical differences when growing up and was also witness to the effect that bullying had on other people. His father bullied him without knowing it, by attempting to force him to do activities that his father thought they could bond over. It had the opposite effect. McVeigh felt trapped, inadequate, and bullied by his father (Michel and Herbeck 2001, 20). Later in life McVeigh witnessed what he perceived as the bullying of the Iraqi Military by the United States. He felt pity for the soldiers and resented the way the US killed them. It was obvious to him that they were not able to fight back in any meaningful way (Michel and Herbeck 2001, 80).

Asahara was also bullied as a child due to his partial blindness. Not given the chance to adjust, he was moved to a school where he had the physical advantage of partial sight over children with no sight. This led him to become a bully, reflecting the life lessons that he had been taught (Lifton 2000, 14). Asahara would continue to use bullying through mental and physical means for the remainder of his time in charge of Aum Shinrikyo. He also learned to reward obedience as well as punish offenders.

71

Khan, Lindsay, and Hussain also suffered some form of bullying as children. Khan and Hussain were bullied as children for no reason at all (House of Commons 2006, 13); they learnt to run away and did not retaliate at all. Lindsay was bullied by his stepfather and was not able to retaliate due to his smaller size and lack of physical ability (House of Commons 2006, 17). All three of them saw the UK's participation in the Iraq and Afghanistan wars as the bullying of those states and the bullying of Islam by Christianity (Randstorp 2010, 105).

Administrative Failure

All members of the case studies felt a perceived or actual failure in the administrative architecture of the state. McVeigh felt that the government was moving against its citizens through the erosion of civil rights, particularly the Second Amendment. Provocative literature coupled with distortion of true events such as Waco and Ruby Ridge allowed McVeigh to fill in the missing pieces and conclude that the government was about to suspend all citizen rights (Michel and Herbeck 2001, 118-120). Internationally McVeigh felt that the UN was working with the corrupt US Government to force other obligations on its citizens and repeal the Second Amendment. This led to McVeigh thinking that he was required to start an uprising against the government (Michel and Herbeck 2001, 126).

Asahara felt that the entire world had failed and that the world needed a new start. His apocalyptic vision said that the majority of the world had lost its way. Asahara was convinced that he would be the catalyst for this new world order through Aum Shinrikyo (Jones 2008, 75).

Khan and the other members of the London bombings cell felt that that their country was at war with their faith and that they were required to defend their faith at all costs. The UK's Government was to blame for the poor housing, lack of facilities for migrants, and the two illegal wars that were being fought in Iraq and Afghanistan (Randstorp 2010, 106). The cell thought that they were obligated by their faith to fight back.

Violence

The final part of the summary is the lesson that all members learnt of violence being a problem solver in life. McVeigh did attempt to use other, nonviolent means before he turned to violence. His letter writing and media interviews show a frustrated man who cannot get his message heard by the right people (Michel and Herbeck 2001, 98-99). He did see a lot of violence work as a tool while he was in the Army, not only through the actions of the Army on the battlefield but through the actions of some of the African Americans in the barracks (Michel and Herbeck 2001, 87). He also saw the government use violence against the people in Waco and Ruby Ridge without any repercussions. In the end he felt that violence was the only way to get his point across.

Asahara extended his childhood bullying tactics into violence as he got older. His use of violence over other children extended to the beating of a customer and then to the killing of followers and dissenters (Lifton 2000, 17). The lack of consequences for his actions at each stage led to him feel that violence was an appropriate tool to use in achieving his aims.

The London bombings cell was also able to identify with violence. They saw the current wars as a tool of the Christian governments and how it was killing thousands of

Muslims. In the lectures from Hamza they heard about the use of violence by other extremists around the world and how it had worked to stop those governments from participating in Iraq and Afghanistan (Randstorp 2010, 105). For Khan and Tanweer they either participated in or saw the effects of violence in Pakistan and perhaps Afghanistan first hand and as noted by the source document experiences, a profound change in attitude upon their return (Rai 2007, 46-47).

Recommendations

This study recommends that democracies should enter into a debate; concerning whether their various versions of civil rights are still relevant and if for the greater good they should be amended to reflect the changing threat against them. It is acknowledged that any restrictions placed upon these rights may cause dissent. However, it is unlikely that countries which subscribe and follow the current set of rights would use this as an excuse to change their political and judicial systems to allow for a suspension of all human rights. Conversely, countries which ignore human rights would probably continue to do so.

Incidents of bullying in schools should automatically result in some form of compulsory police notification or involvement. All of the terrorists experienced bullying in schools and its effect on them can be clearly seen through later life. By tracking the effects of bullying against individuals and maintaining a record, at risk individuals could be identified especially if they become the bullies later in life. It would also force the school system to punish bullies and set a clear example for the victims and prospective perpetrators, that society does not condone that behavior.

The state must be more careful when dealing with problems of national significance. Controversial topics such as war or the right to life will divide different sections of the population into groups, but there must be a clear delineation between a peaceful protest based on coherent arguments with some factual detail and the use of anarchy or violence to achieve their aims. The use of the latter tactics must be quickly stopped and the perpetrators punished swiftly. As each act tends to get progressively more spectacular and violent, it is vital to have a clear delineation between what is acceptable and what will not be tolerated.

The use of violence to solve problems by both the state and the individual must be prevented when reasonably possible. Part of this is striking the balance between a reasonable protest and the state's response. This should be at a point where violence will not be required to halt or disperse the protest. When a state chooses to use violence against another state, it must ensure that proportionality is used to prevent aggrieved parties from feeling that violence is their only option of recourse against the state. Whenever possible, a state should seek concurrence of its population through fair and open discourse, to allow a majority to make an informed decision and the remainder to understand the reasons without being required to resort to violence.

Further Research Topics

There are many areas that require further research to fully understand and exploit the data that could eventually be used to prevent or identify at risk areas. The demography of certain places could allow town planners to prevent the kind of conditions from forming that would allow for the relatively easy radicalization of community members. It would also allow for law enforcement and intelligence collection agencies to target certain areas, based on factors other than ethnicity or religious affiliation.

The first area for further study would be the economic conditions that exist around confirmed homegrown terrorists. Comparing the economic conditions of the areas and even the country, against the economic stature of the individual may establish if personal wealth is a factor in a person's decision to become a terrorist.

Another area requiring further research is the establishment of ethnic enclaves against the majority racial backdrop of a country. Are there correlations between where races and ethnicities decide to reside, or are forced to reside, and violence? The overall ethnic map of a country could be compared to demographic and economic data to see if there are correlations with the attacks and terrorists.

Another area for further research area for study would be to analyze the immigration patterns of persons moving to a Western democracy from a non-western democracy. Research could chart where the majority of ethnicities moved from for the previous two generations and look at the fundamental lifestyle differences, to include such factors as religious and cultural dimensions. Do people transitioning between the two require either long or short term additional assistance to make a successful change? Such research would assist in countries committing to a successful multicultural program with greater surety and safety.

The final new area of research could be into the effects of bullying on first and second generation immigrants. Extensive data has been collected on people who have committed various crimes and links established to traumatic events in their childhood. They are often blamed for contributing to their eventual acts yet no work has been done

76

to see the effects of racial or ethnic based bullying on potential homegrown terrorists. This work would be significant as it would allow authorities to establish at risk groups and individuals.

This research could also be expanded to cover more case studies to establish if the findings remain true over a wider sample range. Recent cases such as the Fort Hood shootings and the planned attack on the Holsworthy Army Base by Australian Somalis could be used to widen the results and confirm or deny through the use of a wider sample.

Conclusion

The findings in this study suggest that democracies have made themselves like a fortress to outsiders. But due to the inherent participation and transparency requirements, democratic government processes remain trusting and engaged with their populations. Terrorists and cells based outside of a democracy would find it hard to get past the numerous security checks required to enter a democracy, but they can export ideas and teachings without many problems.

Homegrown terrorists already exist behind the walls of the democracy. Because the state spends so much time, money, and resources looking for outward threats trying to gain entry, there is relative lack of scrutiny inside the democracy. Coupled with a participative system of government; where everybody is given equal say, is afforded equal rights, and there are numerous checks and balances built into each layer of bureaucracy to ensure that these rights are not tarnished, a democracy can become a perfect place to hide.

It is unclear if any of the members set out with all of their rights in the forefront of their mind and then attempted to use them as cover for their eventual acts. But they were aware of some of their rights. McVeigh was obsessed with his Second Amendment rights and the influence that he thought the government was having on his life. His use of this right and his defense of it eventually led to his act of terrorism. Asahara actively used the right of freedom of thought, conscience, and religion, primarily to make money and recruit new members. In the end it also protected him against an aggressive police investigation because they were fearful on the ramifications if they were incorrect. The members of the London bombing cell were probably not aware of any of their rights, although their preacher Abu Hamza was. Hamza is well aware of his rights as he has been facing deportation for eight year to the US. All the while he has been preaching about the downfall of the UK and the US. His ability to preach hate, under the loose guide of religion has been backed by the judicial system.

A Western style democracy, with it protections and rights is a very noble system but it also allows dissenters. Once they are inside the democracy they are able to easily undermine it and to use violence to attempt to change it. While some of these rights could be changed to prevent these insiders, or homegrown terrorists from acting it would change the nature of the democracy and perhaps turn it from a democracy to a totalitarian state.

www.ingramcontent.com/pod-product-compliance
Lightning Source LLC
Chambersburg PA
CBHW081328310526
45789CB00018B/2592